UNDERSTANDING DEATH

D1286952

Understanding
Death

Evelyn Francis Capel

First published as *Death, The End is the Beginning*, 1979
Reprinted 1987
This edition 1990

British Library Cataloguing in Publication Data
Capel, Evelyn Francis
Death
1. Death   Religious aspects   Christianity
I. Title
248.4   BT825

ISBN 0-904693-04-X

Published by Temple Lodge Press,
51 Queen Caroline Street, London W6 9QL, England

Typeset by DP Photosetting, Aylesbury
Printed by Billing & Sons Ltd, Worcester

To my dear friend
Nancy Kennard
in deep respect for her
work with the dying.

Contents

Foreword

'Do it yourself' is today's motto. It is as true of living one's life as of doing all kinds of jobs. But what are the instructions? The art of living is changing, and has changed, because the human situation is changing. Here are, not instructions, but comments on the patterns of life that are emerging.

The sacraments to which reference is made are those celebrated in the Christian Community, a new movement for the development of Christianity. Sacraments are that which express the spiritual dignity of human existence.

1
Thinking about Death

Death enfolds the mystery of love.

The eternal soul in each one of us came at birth from the Universe, leaving the place of origin, the true home. To die is to return there. The love of home moves the soul to go. Is there ever, at the very last stage reluctance to leave? The soul will be reluctant to leave those who are loved here, but not to take the way home again.

The love of God for each individual soul is revealed at death more than ever before. When there is no interference in the process of dying, the moment of the final breath and heartbeat is divinely appointed. In death the soul, called back to the Heavens by the Father, and filled with the love of God, accepts the divine invitation to come home.

In the face of death the love existing between people shines out in its true divine character. Liking and disliking, attraction and repulsion are left behind. The person in dying sees the eternal in other people just as he becomes aware of it in himself. A touch of death illumines all true love, just as an intimation of the immortal most truly reveals the mortal. The dignity of man is felt in death. In whatever way dying is nowadays degraded, however much fear clouds its mystery, the experience is there of going towards the light, of going home.

Some realistic suggestions are offered here about handling situations which arise though death. They are presented in a brief style, because those who will need them will want them there and then. There is bound to be a sense of emergency. Had Rudolf Steiner* in this century not made plain how the human soul partakes in two worlds, both equally real, such suggestions could not have been put so distinctly.

* The Austrian-born founder of Anthroposophy (1861-1925).

2
Facing Death

The mystery of life deepens both at its beginning and at its end. We come and we go! From where do we come? To what are we bound? At either end of the way there is the door and the unanswered question.

It can be said of death that it is the other appearance of birth, just as birth is of death. It is the end that is also the beginning. It is the encounter of the higher self with the oridinary person to whom he is bound. The ordinary self stood in front until now, an identity with name and address. He retires to be a memory. But the true self, the person known by the insight of love, emerges triumphant. It is the real, the lasting one, who is not lost but made known in death.

To die is to make and to put into practice a decision. Once upon a time another decision had been made. The eternal soul looked earthwards and resolved to descend. He could never have done so on his own. He had helpers around him who were protecting and leading him to the path of his true destiny. They could see as only angels, archangels, and the company of Heaven can see. They urged the decision. The higher self made it. This portion of the eternal being has thus stood back from earth existence. It has continued to stand at the threshold, while the personality has come right through into life here. Thereby it has made and keeps the link with the spiritual Universe so that the contact with our true and spiritual home is never lost. The higher self remains embraced within the living, moving Will of God. It can direct the decision to be born and, later on, the will to die. It shines like a star into the soul of the ordinary person living his daily life.

The body is the house which the soul inhabits on earth. As little as a person would entirely identify himself with the house in which he lives, so little can he maintain that his body is himsélf.

The soul has entered the house of the body with the first breath and will go out again with the last breath. Being born is a process of breathing in. Dying is the process of breathing out, for the last time. The earliest drawing of the young child is most often that of the house, with roof, windows, doors and chimney, all projecting his experience of entering his first house, which becomes his original dwelling. To die means to leave the house which, bit by bit, he has made into his own. In the larger sense it means to leave the place on earth in which he has become aware of himself, has had his experience, and has been able to do his work. Coming near to death rouses in the heart a strong awareness of work done and left undone. On leaving its house the soul looks back to what life within it has meant, constructing a picture of the person who has been living in that house. At the core of the soul is the self. The soul is involved in the process of dying, of which it is first made aware by the free higher self who is not involved with ordinary human considerations. The self is not really of this world, in fact one part of its being, the higher self, never in truth leaves the world of God, but has come to dwell for a while in the house with a spiritual sense of purpose. From the higher wisdom of the world of God the call comes to the self to return. The self is represented in that world by a star, which shines over him when he is down in the house of the body. So the higher self is seen. The star calls and he must go. On his part the decision is made to answer the call. The process of dying, be it long or short, is the carrying out of the decision in the region of the soul and body.

3
In the Event of a Death

No one, said Florence Nightingale, should be left to die alone.
As far as possible, a dying person should not be left alone, even
when there is nothing to do in a practical way. The loving
presence is what he needs. The companion may be quiet, even
silent. There may or may not be need for talking and doing.
Listening and responding is more appropriate.

Attitude of mind

It is wise to keep clearly in one's thoughts the fact that one is
standing beside a person who is approaching the threshold to the
new life, which will be found in the spiritual world. It is useful to
make an imaginative picture of this reality, in the form of either a
gate that is opening, a curtain that is being drawn aside, or a
horizon which opens out into the distance. It is not necessary to
speak about the picture. It will work strongly as an unspoken
thought.

Coming to meet the soul who is journeying towards the
threshold is the figure of Christ. We die with Him. Even those
souls who have not sought the experience of Christianity have the
meeting with Him at death. Thus should one think, when keeping
company with the dying.

A very intense personal relationship can arise between the one
who is dying and the companion. A particular kind of love, which
illumines with the light like that of a sunset, shines out. It is
personal , yet more than that. Souls recognise each other in the
ideal of their humanity, without the need to form a relationship in
terms of daily life. It is both one of the most real of all kinds of love
and the most free, being relieved of egotism. It enriches the heart.

It should be acknowledged with openness of mind in the companion's behaviour.

Such an attitude will bring inspirations of the right kind about what should be said and done. The wishes of the one who is dying should be accepted as outer expressions of inner experience. It is not necessary to be alarmed by the signs of struggle, which often appear towards the end. The soul is engaged in pulling away from the body, which as an experience seen from within, is in contrast to that which it appears to be from without. Some dying people cry out or try to leave the bed. The death rattle itself is a process by which the soul is expelled from the body. The soul which was breathed in at birth is breathing itself out. The struggle is taking place for another kind of birth. Help and support, given without fear, are the final gift which one person can give to another.

What can be said to the dying

It will often be more valuable to listen and reply than to say much oneself. The dying person is usually not able to grasp thoughts which he has not understood earlier. He will be inclined towards looking back over his destiny and over the relationship which he has had to other people. He will in fact be gathering the harvest of the life time which is closing. The experience will often be reflected in what he says and asks. Although he is ending his life here, his thoughts will be directed towards a new beginning. When he begins to speak of what he is going to do or of doing over again better what he has tried to do earlier, then the mood of death is upon him. Such resolutions for the future should be supported and encouraged. They are a true expression of his feeling that in the ending of one life there is the beginning of another.

Should someone be told that he is dying? In the depths of his heart he will know that he is entering into death. The decision to die has been made between God and his higher self. But the process by which the conscious, personal mind grasps the knowledge of the decision may take time. In reality, a person has to tell himself that he is dying. Unless he asks the question of someone else which he is really asking himself, the answer has little meaning. He grasps it only when he is ready to do so. The companion is not obliged to feel that he must tell him, for he may well not really know. Until the moment of death has actually come, it is very hard to judge when someone will die. The companion may assume that death is inevitable. He may have been told so on medical authority. Even this is presumed, rather than known.

The fear of death

An experience of fear is an inevitable stage in the process of dying, which is sometimes, nevertheless, to be avoided. The capacity to fear is built into the human constitution. It is encountered by the soul on coming into the body at birth. It has to be passed through again on the way out of the body at death. In a smaller way it is known throughout life in the form of the jitters which are often experienced on important occasions. It should not be a cause for shame but it asks for comfort. The biggest events in our human existence are birth and death, the coming and going. How should the soul not know fear and awe?

A part of the transformation taking place in death is the parting with the double. A parasite of soul, a personal devil accompanies each person from the time of birth until just before death. The double tends to represent the personality in the form of a caricature, which is carried around all through life, even when the conscious character is full of good qualities. It can cause caricatures of behaviour when the conscious personality loses control. The double can be reluctant to leave the soul whom he has known for so long. Struggles and expressions of fear may be manifested as the double is compelled to withdraw. When the process is completed, the true nobility of character shines forth. To be with someone when he is freed from his double is to have a clear experience of the beautiful nature that is his. The companion will feel a sense of blessing descending upon himself.

What can be read to the dying

When someone is very sick and finding it difficult to concentrate, fairy stories and legends will often give help and pleasure. The imaginative pictures will occupy the mind with the kind of wisdom that strengthens the soul without causing intellectual strain. The most valuable of all reading is from the Bible. It is most useful to choose passages which the dying person knows well and has loved. He needs to bring the memory of the wisdom, that he has learnt before, to meet what he hears in the extremity. It is equally true of any reading which is offered to the dying outside of the Gospels. What has been known and loved before will give the greatest strength and comfort.

Certain passages from the Gospels are particularly appropriate. The story of Christ walking on the water to meet the apostles in the darkness of night is one, especially including the words: 'It is I; be not afraid' (St John 6). Another is the raising of Lazarus (St John 11). Chapter 15 of St John is valuable in the hour of death and most of all Chapter 17, which describes the prayer of Christ to the Father for the souls of those who have come to Him.

Prayers

The prayer that has been known and loved before is worth most at death. The original and universal Christian prayer is that which Christ taught to those who followed Him, the Lord's Prayer. It is always of the greatest value in death as in life. For those who have loved the Bible, Psalm 23 may be very suitable. A prayer for inner peace and one for finding the meaning of life are true in the hour of death. Here are examples:

> Spirit-Light.
> Bountiful
> Strengthening
> Quickening
> Into me
> Pours.

> In the beginning was Christ
> and Christ was with the Gods
> And a God was Christ.
> Deep in each human soul
> Being of Christ indwells,

In my soul too He dwells
And He will lead me
To the true meaning of my life.

(Rudolf Steiner)

After death has already taken place, a prayer should be said for the soul that is entering the Universe.

Angels, archangels and archai
in the weaving of the etheric
receive the web of the destiny

or

Into the hands of Christ
be committed this soul
that He may bear it up
into the realms of the Father.

What can be done

Death is something holy. The room is which the death takes place and where the body lies is a sanctuary. It can be decorated for this purpose. Candles should burn there. The flame of the candle gives the comforting light which the dying person can appreciate. Flowers through their colour, scent and the feeling they represent speak to the heart, both before and after death. Pictures and things of beauty from nature, such as minerals, belong in the room. Any symbols that have carried a sacred meaning for the one who has died, or for the people round, should be used. Supposing that the body can be kept in such a room for the three days that should elapse until the funeral, this kind of decoration should be kept until the body has been taken away. Lighting candles, saying prayers and reading such passages as have been described, can be continued when possible at suitable intervals throughout this time.

In most religions and Christian Churches there are services for the dying. Efforts should always be made to hold them, even when the person who is dying has not appeared to set great store by religion. In the Christian Community a new form of service called the Anointing is held for the dying. A description is given on page 15. It is necessary for those who are caring for the sick person to request that this service be held before the death has actually taken place. Such a decision is often felt to be hard to make. But in calmness of mind its right moment will be found. Should the patient take a turn for the better after the service, which can certainly happen, he will only benefit from having received it.

> The sun in your heart shall glow
> The stars round your head shall sound,
> The moon shall uphold from below,
> The earth shall give firm ground.
>
> Holding up high your head
> Stretching your hands out wide,
> Your feet shall surely tread
> With the grace of God to guide.

4
Care for the Dying

'The right to live is a fundamental human right.' At the present time this is put forward as the most fundamental of all rights. But it is constantly challenged with legal arguments and by behaviour. Who has the right to kill? Who kills today because of the might of the gun in his hand without any thought of rights? The problem is now twofold. There are violent people who kill for reasons of their own, which in the last resort may be purely an impulse to violence which finds no restraint from within. There are those likewise, who for reasons regarded as humanitarian, out of goodwill, argue the point of whether the lives of others may be taken. Out of their thinking the phrase 'mercy killing' or 'Euthanasia' has been coined to give a talking point. It is debated whether someone with an incurable disease can request to be put to death by medical means or whether he should be cared for until death comes to meet him in the course of nature. The problem is further complicated by the discovery of drugs which can be used to prolong by artificial means a life that would under its own conditions come to an end. Who is to decide when they are to be used? The patient is very unlikely to be in a condition to be asked. When a conference was held not long ago in London on these problems its theme was entitled 'Care for the Dying'. Life or death were seen in the practical light of what the process of dying in fact means. It was clearly felt that this should be faced before that of the rights and wrongs of euthanasia. It was the first time that a large public was willing to discuss openly such questions with those who had both medical and religious experience.

Dying

Dying is the inevitable conclusion of every lifetime. He who is born will have to die. Why is it then that for such a long period dying has been pushed out of the usual attitude to living? Why in a hospital is death so often felt as a defeat? Why, as a doctor once pointed out, does a British death certificate have to state a cause of death for which the realistic phrase 'just died' is not accepted. It would seem that death is assumed to be an extraordinary event brought about by some external cause. It is spoken of in some circles as a kind of weakness; in a village for instance, where retired people have gone to live, a neighbour might be heard to say concerning the end of a life: 'the silly woman went and died.'

That many people are willing to speak openly about the care of the dying means that these old attitudes are changing. They had their origin in fear. Death has not at all times been felt to be a barrier to life. William Blake could draw a picture of a dead body on a bier with the soul rising above it as a separate being looking back in astonished grief at the body from which it had been parted. Blake was an exception in his own time but this picture would have been readily understood by those who lived before the great uprush of the intellectual powers of the mind which produced the Renaissance and the Reformation. Such powers gave to people in Europe a new ability to deal with the things of this world and darkened their minds for that which belongs to the world beyond death. The more capable and interested people became in earthly existence, the more uncertain they became about the spiritual world so that the person who had established himself in personality and position would ultimately find himself unable to imagine himself existing after death. Would he lose or would he gain by dying? Surely he would lose? Such a fundamental question became pushed out of ordinary life to enter the dim religious light in which by now people walked only on special occasions. What is not faced becomes a source of dread and the problem of death has lived on unrecognised in modern times because it brings with it a sense of defeat.

In this century, through the work of Rudolf Steiner the picture of the spiritual universe can be taken into the minds of modern people by their own power to consider and to think. The dark curtain hanging over the experiences of sleep and of the life beyond death can be lifted. Grief does not disappear but unreasonable dread can be overcome. So that it no longer becomes necessary to take evading action before the problem of dying.

Birth in death

Behind the question of what is the right kind of care to give to the dying, stands another. What does the process of dying mean for the one who is involved in it? An old lady, whose daughters were trying to soothe her on her death bed, said to them sternly: 'What do you think, dying is very hard work'. Experiences shows that it can just as well be regarded as a kind of labour as the process of birth for which this word is commonly used. Spirit, soul and body have been living together for a long time. The body has become unable to maintain the house for the soul. They must part. Unless death takes place by violence, the process can be a long struggle passing through different stages each with its own symptoms. Those who gather round may experience distress at the changes in breathing and at the restlessness. Some dying people call out that they want to go home, or try with their last strength to get up and move. When there is pain the bystanders may be very anxious for the use of drugs that suppress the symptoms of the process. What in fact is happening is a labour in which the comfort and help of those around is much required.

It is the labour of the soul and spirit to emerge from the grave of the dying body and be born into the new life beyond death. The help and comfort that are to be given are most effective when they are offered out of this understanding. The sick person is emerging from illness and suffering as he dies. He is pulling away from his destiny on earth and its troubles. He is separating from that in his personality which has been weak, fearful and wrong. He is rising into his true being of spirit with its noble intentions and true ideals. He is being born into the light of the spiritual Universe. But he is leaving behind the familiar existence in the body and transcending his old self. How can this be anything but a dramatic process of severe change? But is not the purpose of those who are with the dying to help in every way to make the change triumphant? Should they not avoid trying to obscure the labour to avoid distress for themselves?

When dying is understood as being the means by which the spirit and soul are born into a new existence there will be the courage to face every stage as part of the whole. The death of loved ones is always grievous, especially when there is the fear that in undergoing so great a change our relationship to them is in danger of being lost. Death is change for those who die and for those who remain here. Yet in every process inspired by the spirit, change must come.

Consciousness

How far is it valuable to try to spare the one who is dying the awareness of what is happening to him? Is the dramatic shock of the change which he is undergoing too much for him to face? This question arises as much for those who are around him as for the one himself. What is the difference between facing a great event and evading it through pretence or the help of tranquillisers? Within each human soul there dwells the spirit or true self. It is distinct from the personality which is the bearer of fears, weaknesses and wishes. It is the hero hidden within the unheroic character. At death the personality is gradually dissolved and the self emerges as the immortal part. If for the sake of the weakness of the personality great experiences are avoided the heroic self is hindered in its growth. When, in spite of the personality the self rises to courage the true process of development can happen. The loving companions of one who is dying can perceive his true self very often more clearly in the last stage of the lifetime than they could earlier. Love of a kind that transcends limitation can shine out between those who meet at a death bed, not only in the last hours but even for weeks before. It is one of the soundest reasons for holding the view that dying people should realise their condition that they will thereby be able to enter knowingly into loving relationships of this kind with those who are around them. When everyone knows there need be no pretence. There can be the appreciation, which those have for each other, who are sharing the great experience of the triumph of the spirit over its need for the body and the limitation of the personality. Anyone who stays away from a death bed because of distress, because the physical aspects of illness can be so very unpleasant will turn out to have missed the one experience of a lifetime, which can make known the true heights of love.

If the one who is dying is permitted to remain as conscious as his natural condition will allow he may pass through many stages of experience, some of them distressful, but the power of his true self will grow, becoming more able to face the experience of death. He will need, when he has crossed the threshold, all the strength of selfhood which he has gathered in the process of facing the great change of death knowingly. We are very much aware of who we are in this world with the help given by the body. It is the house in which spirit and soul dwell, knowing themselves to be at home, where they belong. Without the body the self has to establish another means of self-consciousness. The moment of death clearly known can act as a beacon illuminating the consciousness of being a self long after the time has passed. Rudolf Steiner, in speaking of the experiences of people who have died, which he was able to trace, could state as a real piece of information that the well-being of someone who has died is much enhanced through the effort of consciousness with which death has been faced. Though it may seem in one sense kind to blur the experience of death on this side, the effect is the opposite on the other side of the threshold.

The strongest motive for giving drugs to the sick and dying is to spare them, as one hopes, the suffering of pain, but this is no simple matter. It is difficult to judge how much pain another person is in fact feeling. Drugs may easily be given far in excess of what is required or continue to be administered as a matter of habit. It is good to know that at a recent conference in London, a larger public was made aware that research is being done in some hospitals, caring for the dying, into the relationship between pains of different kinds and the means of alleviating them. Much more skill in handling pain and in preserving consciousness should come about by this means. A more obscure form of suffering which is at present easily overlooked would then be readily considered. The drugged patient who seems to lie quiet can be suffering nightmares induced by the drugs from which he will be struggling in misery to escape. Yet the people around will be quite unaware that they are in fact taking him out of one trouble into another. A further danger of this obscure type arises when a patient appears to have become unconscious without drugs, perhaps fallen into a coma, and the bystanders believe that he is insensitive to what they feel and say. This is a dangerous illusion. The patient who cannot speak can still hear and is far more sensitive than he ever was to the thoughts of those beside him. It is always valuable to pray beside the unconscious person. Loving words sent to him will not be wasted. A visit to someone who is said not to know that the visitor is there is never lost.

The Anointing

The spiritual and the earthly life meet at the death-bed. The religious care for the dying is equally important as the medical. Even those who expect to deal with their ordinary affairs without much concern for religion will feel that it is needed in the hour of death. As much skill is required to handle the process of dying in a religious way as through nursing. At some time during the process, in the early stage and not the later one, the patient who is able to talk may feel the need to look back over his past life. He will want to do this as if he were looking from outside and he will be thinking with spiritual insight. He will feel the need to be listened to, not just by a friend, but by a pastor who understands the care of souls, who will meet him with spiritual discernment. On the other hand the mere desire to soothe will not be adequate. The pastor will help more by wise listening than by anything which he himself would say. People in the process of dying cannot take in what they have not thought earlier. But they need to be understood with the same kind of wisdom with which they themselves can look back over a lifetime. The threshold between this life and the next is a place of insight near to that of God. It is never soothing for the dying to be diverted by good cheer.

The sacrament which belongs to the great and solemn transformation of death is the Anointing. The substance in use is olive oil, taken from the olives which ripen on the branches of the tree, spreading themselves out in the sunshine. There is a strong quality of sun's warmth in the oil of the olive which is a link between heaven and earth. The holy oil, consecrated for the purpose is used for making three signs of the cross on the forehead of the dying person. Such an action eases the passing of the soul away from the body and brings peace into the labour of dying. The words of Christ in which He prayed to the Father for the souls of men are read. In this sacrament, the one who is dying becomes aware that he is making a decision out of the strength of his true self, that he is not being forced from the body but is deciding to leave with his own will. He is not choosing his own death or deciding when to go. But he is making a decision in co-operation with the will of God. He can say: 'Thy will be done', for this is now his will likewise. The element of decision is always present at death but it can be obscured behind reactions of many kinds. The spiritual strength of the soul is greatly increased when the decision is taken into the conscious mind, not because the dying person has been told by someone else from outside, but because in the sacrament the true self can come to know his own mind.

At the gate of death every soul meets Christ. In the sacrament of the Anointing the light of this meeting shines clearly into the heart. Without it, the meeting though real may be obscured. Why should Christ come to meet even those who have not looked for His presence during life? The transformation undergone at death is the process of joining together the heavenly and earthly part of human nature. That which has ripened during the lifetime on earth is to be gathered up and carried into the life of the spiritual Universe without being lost. At the present time no one is able without spiritual help to link together what he has been on earth and will be in Heaven. Christ comes to the soul, in labour to be born again, as the great helper of the birth into the divine world.

5
Ways of Dying

Sudden death

When death comes slowly and quietly, the process of dying can be accompanied in the way already described. The original pattern is set out clearly under such circumstances. But death comes in many other ways bringing the question; what is to be done now? Sudden death can strike, without preparation, in the midst of life, through the manifold kinds of accidents to which we are prone at the present time. Every new invention brings its own kind of disaster with it. Technical advances produce a greater variety of accidents. Sudden death is a daily affair in modern life. It used to be thought necessary to pray to be spared its shock. It was felt that to go slowly and quietly was a better way of dying, but today there is another attitude.

Shock is the essence of the experience, both for the one who dies and for those in the surroundings. The practical question will be how to behave under the impact of the shock. The one who dies will experience a forceful awakening of consciousness. One moment the soul is aware of the world of the earth, and in the next the real, powerful world of the spirit is opened before his gaze. He is initiated into the knowledge of the spiritual world with violence. He experiences the call from one life to the next as the direct intervention of the power of God. Can it be said that a shock of this kind is a disaster? Is the divine mercy not at work, for the sake of the spiritual powers that will grow in the soul out of such an experience?

The companions, whether they are present at the accident or only involved later, encounter both the shock to themselves and to the one who dies. If the natural fear can be overcome, then the presence of the spirit can be felt with strength-giving power. The prayers that can be prayed may be only short, but they can be very powerful.

The first thought should be for the guardian angel. The good will of the heart should be directed towards him, to add human strength to that with which the angel supports and uplifts the departing soul. Thought should further be given to the presence of Christ, who is always to be encountered at the Gate of Death, the more strongly because the experience is so concentrated. Further still the thought should reach towards the being of the Father in the Heavens, who will take the soul up into the fullness of His Being on the other side of the Gate. If there is no time for more, it is still of great worth to call in this manner upon the Trinity. A picture can be formed like this: Carried by the spirit this soul is passing into the hands of Christ, who brings him to the realm of the Father. The sign of the Cross can rightly be made.

The prayers and readings which were described earlier can be appropriately used for someone who dies suddenly, either in the presence of the body or without it, according to what is allowed by the circumstances. The moment of death releases the soul from depending on the body for communicating with other people. Suddenly they know each other soul to soul, spirit to spirit, in a clear interchange of thought and goodwill. Such a condition is discovered for a short time clearly and confidently under the impact of the shock. The sacrament of the Anointing is intended to be held at a deathbed. When there is no such thing, the words of the sacrament can be read. They will still be that which the dying soul needs to hear. Something must nevertheless be missing, the signs which should be made with the fingers on the forehead of the body that is being left behind. But the words can be offered by those, who are able to gather round, to the support and comfort of the dying soul, and for the sake of working with the angels. This is so, even if no body can be reached. Sudden death calls for behaviour of a special kind, but not for omitting what would otherwise be done under easier conditions.

Violent death

To be killed by another person or other people is not only to die with shock, but by the hand of enemies. Everyone concerned is faced with moral experiences of an acute kind, added to the shock of death itself. That which belongs most essentially to the person himself, his life on earth, has been taken away from him by the will-forces of others. How does he see this in death? It will be important to pray that he may look upon what is happening to him with the eyes of Christ. If the soul is involved with impulses of hate and revenge, the suffering will be greater. If the soul realises how helpless the murderers are in the grip of impulses of evil, he may be consoled by feelings of compassion, but he will need to find the help and courage of Christ to face those powers which have attacked him. Still further, he will find in the heart of Christ the powers that will transform the grim experience into powers of soul which will be used for creating what is good. Prayers which call most particularly on the healing power of Christ should be prayed not once, but over a long period of time. It would be advisable to read for the sake of someone who has died violently, the story of the Crucifixion from St Luke's Gospel. Thoughts of those, who have commited violence, and who are entangled in their deed, could well be brought to the act of reading. The words of Christ spoken from the Cross are deeds of transformation. There flows from them the divine strength to change the forces of hate, suffering and death into the living power of love. They are the roses of the spirit that blossom from the Cross. In such a picture the story of the Crucifixion can be offered as a means of healing.

Suicide

The person who has taken away from himself that which was given to him at birth by the spiritual world, his life on earth, brings suffering upon himself. It should be said at this point that no individual case should be hastily judged to be true suicide, even though someone has obviously done violence to himself. The appearance and the reality may well be different. It is wise to leave the question open of whether the person who has died was perhaps a victim of forces that he could not control, such as those of tremendous fear or of mental disease. The suicide as such will go for a period through the experience of being an outcast. He cannot immediately be received into the spheres of the Universe, because his time has not yet come. He has deprived himself of his place on earth and will suffer for a time the pain of desolation. The comfort of loving thoughts and prayers will be his need. If he can be given a place in the hearts of people whom he has known, the experience of being an outcast will be eased. It will by its nature last for a certain length of time until finally the soul is freed to begin the journey of the life after death. Those who have kept their contact with the one who has died will feel reflected in their hearts his passage from the darkness into the light.

Reading from the Gospels is a reliable means of bringing experiences of light to those who have died. The passage which could especially do so in the desolation of suicide is the story of the raising of Lazarus in St John's Gospel. It is an example of how the life on earth is seen through the eyes of Christ. The meaning of life on earth is expressed in the words: 'I am the resurrection and the life'. To hear these words in the heart is to know the meaning of the courage needed to live a lifetime upon the earth. They can bring healing to the fear of existence.

Death in youth

Those who die young take with them all the forces that have not been exhausted in the years of a long life. Those who are left behind here may well feel painfully the loss of those years which had not been filled. But on the other side of existence, other realities are to be found. Seeds for the future are sown in the souls of those who have early to leave their life on earth. In praying for them it is of particular value to see in thought the meaning of that part of earth evolution which is still to come. In St John 21 the resurrection is described, first as it was seen by Mary Magdalene in the morning, and then by the apostles in the evening. It is set out in the narrative as a process beginning on Easter day and stretching on into the distances of time. Such a vision of history can be offered to the soul that has left the earth after a short stay, to bring meaning into all our striving for the future. It is necessary to be able to look back to the earth with hope, if the will shall be actively directed towards that which has still to be done in times to come. The precious offering which those take who go young into death is their fresh force of will for the ideals to which their hearts have been devoted. Enthusiasm which has never been worn out is theirs.

Death in childhood

The pain most severely felt in modern times comes from the experience of death in childhood. Whether a baby is born dead, dies a little later, or lives into the years of childhood, it is still the saddest of griefs when the soul leaves this world after only a short stay. Gone are the days when it was a matter of course that many who were born did not grow up. It is now expected that every child will reach maturity. There is no way of diminishing the tragedy of failure that early death seems to represent in modern times.

Is it in fact so that every child that is born is meant to grow up? Should it not be considered that a human soul might enter bodily existence and not need to stay for a lifetime to achieve that for which it came. Should not the manifold needs of many different souls be considered? Each person clearly comes into this world with intentions that are only and entirely his. How can each one be required to follow the same pattern when his destiny is quite individual? Should not the thought be allowable that a child who dies has come with a purpose that has already been fulfilled? Are not the forces of childhood a remarkable offering to take through the Gate of Death? May not the soul be glad not to have outgrown the wonder and confidence of childhood, and to be able to take them directly into the life beyond the Gate of Death?

It is hard for those involved with the death of a child to realise that they should not any more think of him only in his childish character. A fully grown spiritual person stands behind every child. The purpose of growing up is that the one who stands behind should be able to come forward and show himself through the body and through the personality, as they enlarge and mature. But such a greater person has been there all the time and has been released at death from the appearance of the child who could contain him only in part. It is easy to remember the little one, with his engaging ways, who is no longer to be seen in the body. But after death the child will not be as he was. He will have become one with the greater person who in fact he has always been. This one has never passed properly through the Gate of Birth. He has looked in for a short time and thus withdrawn.

Although it can be maintained that, for the soul itself death is much less of a dramatic change in childhood, because the process of birth has not been complete, nevertheless the shock and grief will be the greater for parents and other friends. The burden of disappointment that so fair a beginning came so quickly to an end, that the hope of childhood is not to be fulfilled, has to be borne by the parents in particular. They are involved with their own grief but likewise that of their child. However necessary in terms of destiny, in its higher aspect, the short lifetime may be, it is still fraught with the feeling that something has been cut off which should have developed to the full. There is one thought that makes the burden bearable. It comes from the understanding that the decision to die is not made here on earth. It comes from the heart of God Himself. He invites, and the soul leaves the body and passes into the Universe as an invited guest. Has anyone on earth the right to say that the invitation should not have been given? One can only ask to see the higher purpose behind the heavy disappointment, that the death of any child must be.

None of us dies once, but many times, although at long intervals in the course of existence. The soul who takes leave in childhood will be looking at the meaning of having descended to earth, of having been involved even so briefly with the human history of our time. What can be read to meet such an experience? Turning to the Gospels one may look in St Matthew 25 at the parable of the Talents. It describes how earthly people are seen from the divine point of view. They have been offered a place in which to unfold their capacities, that is to say existence on earth in the body. They have been endowed with what they have on loan from God. It is asked of them that they should make more of that which has been given to them, that they should show a return from an outlay. If they can do this, they will be asked to take on bigger responsibilities in the future. In such a way as this, but in many other ways too, a picture of the higher purpose of our life on earth can be shared with the souls of those who have left so early.

It is a strange fact that in our time, when death in childhood is felt to be so tragic, that such a feeling is not extended by everyone to the living child still in the womb. To kill by technical means the unborn child is regarded by some people as quite justified if the social consequences of allowing the child to be born threaten to be unpleasant. How does it come about that in our generation, we are so at odds with ourselves, that so thorough-going a distinction can be made between the born and the unborn baby? Naturally there are many who feel strongly that no distinction can be made. But abortion is still accepted by others who expect to bewail the death of a child once the body has left that of the mother. Do we know where and when to weep in our day?

Death in middle life

Death in old age is accepted as inevitable, as indeed it is. Death at other stages of life carries the flavour of tragedy. Under modern conditions, death is encountered often enough coming between youth and old age, at a time when a person is usually fitted out with a place in the world, with useful work and responsibilities that matter to him and to others. Death in middle life has the strongest impact on the people around who are apt to have depended on the one who leaves, while he is still so much needed. Most commonly it is the father of the family, who is taken by death, while the children are still growing up, his share of the undertaking being left to his widow. But time and time again it is also the women who are taken away before they could be called old.

At the death of an active, vital person, the question may be felt: was he or she really at the end of life, or was there a call from the other side to cut short the natural course of the years? There are needs to be met on the other side of the Gate by those who can take with them energies not exhausted here. There are experiences to which souls can be summoned, whose spiritual advancement takes a dramatic step onward when it might have proceeded in a longer, slower way. All other considerations are swept aside, the soul is raised to higher stages of experience, for purposes that are out of sight for those left behind. It is an observation often to be made today that an illness will set in, which brings with it a prolonged struggle. The sick person passes successfully through the trial, the illness is clearly overcome in soul and body, but death follows. The physical part has been too much destroyed for the body to remain habitable. An important crisis of destiny has been encountered. The soul has been released into new cycles of life through a true victory. But those left behind have to bear the loss. In St John 14 at the opening of the Easter discourses, Christ speaks of the way to the Father, His way, which will also be our way. In these words, the path from our life here on earth to that which begins at death is described by Christ Himself. Here are the thoughts which will meet the experience of those who have to leave this world in the active period of life, when they are most aware of the part that they have here to fulfil.

> Where does the road wend?
> Further than you can see.
> Where does the stream end?
> In the far-distant sea.
> Whither does time extend?
> into Eternity.

6
Care for the Bereaved

Loss

The more someone is loved and needed, the greater the gap he will leave when he is called away. The lives of all those who have known him will be changed. There are two sides to the experience of bereavement. One of them is finding and facing the empty space left behind. The shoes lying in the cupboard, the unworn clothes, the empty chair, the handwriting, that is suddenly a thing of the past, they speak of loss relentlessly. How is it to be faced? There are those who keep the relics together as long as possible, like Queen Victoria who would not allow her husband's bedroom to be changed. There are equally those who move everything away, making a new outer situation promptly. No one can decide which is the better method since it depends on the inclination of those who are involved. But, whichever way is chosen, the problem remains the same, to face the gap which brings a quite new situation for those who are left behind. With the passing of the weeks, new customers will replace the old. Kind people may help the process along. But everything depends on the inner attitude of those most affected by the bereavement. New problems will be bred when attempts are made to cover up and ignore the situation. The old situation has to be touched by the magic of transformation. For no two events are the same. There are deaths meaning the laying down of burdens and the relief from suffering, and there are others that seem like pure loss. But the transforming touch is still valuable, whatever may have happened. Bereavement, for better or for worse means change to be faced and accepted. There is such a thing as active acceptance expressed in the point of view which says: what can be created out of this event, which is a fact to be accepted? But it would be heartless to expect anyone to ask this question at once. The experience of the gap cannot be passed over without the risk of dangerous after effects. In much earlier times than the present, customs were in use through which experiences were lived through and felt through before they were allowed to slip away. It would never have occurred to people of that time that there was any virtue in going on as usual or behaving as if nothing had happened. Today the other attitude is common but full of danger, since the unlived experience will have its revenge. But when the loss has been faced, it is time to do something with it. The feeling for the future can enter in, when the past is allowed to retreat. Where are those things which could not be done before but can be done now? Such a question is a useful starting point. There is a certain skill in waiting for the moment when a question can find its own answer. Here again an experience should be allowed to have its own way. A question should not be asked demanding an immediate answer. Timing is an important part of dealing skillfully with life. In its outer aspect bereavement passes through three stages, the experience of the gap, the accepting of the change, and the willingness to transform the old situation into the new.

Mourning

The inner side of bereavement is mourning. It arises from the sense of an inner gap, just as the feeling of loss arises from the outer gap. The greatest grief is felt where there has been the greatest love. But people have been known to mourn for others whom they did not love or even positively hate. There is an old story of a sanatorium in which two old gentlemen lived for many years at constant variance with one another. But when the one died, the other survived him for only a very short time, for he could not live without his opposite. Some are known to die when their burdens have been removed. The heart can be broken for more reasons than love.

Just as it is true that one should not pass too hastily over the experience of loss, so it is with that of mourning. Grief should have its time and have its way. It can do damage to cheer up a person who has not mourned enough. It is equally unsatisfactory if the experience of grief is prolonged too far. What has begun out of a genuine sense of bereavement can become quite self centred until the reason for grief is overlooked. But if a time of mourning is not lived through the experience either becomes superficial or dangerously deep. It is a matter of skill to offer comfort enough but not too much. No person of proper feelings can avoid grief at the death of someone loved because it is the shadow cast by his love. And all mourning asks for comfort. It is naturally felt that a bereaved person should be visited, given flowers and shown through every kind of token how deeply the others feel with him. Mourning is a social experience in which others will naturally join, even when the old social customs relating to death are in disuse. Grief is a highly personal experience but no one should properly be left alone with it. On the other hand he will suffer if he is jollied out of it before it has run its course.

Mourning people need to be visited and should be allowed to talk about the one for whom they are grieving, remembering what he was like, what he experienced and what part of his intentions was left unfulfilled. There is an old ballad, of which the hero dies in the forest when he is very young. His lament is heard far and wide, with the complaint that his barn has not been built, his corn-field cut, and his babe born. Such may be the grief of someone dying without a sense of fulfilment and those who mourn will be sharing it. Self-centred mourning makes a barrier between those who have stayed behind and the one who has gone ahead. But true grief can be a means of sharing the experience of the one who was loved.

But the time comes when mourning which has been properly experienced should change. A new relationship to the one who has died should be built. It will be formed through the inner effort to share the ideals of the one who has left this world. Those who die do not remain exactly as they were. Death means transcending that which is of the body and of the ordinary, limited personality. The greater nature, in which ideals are cherished, becomes more real as the old personality fades. The custom of the past to see certain qualities of those who have died in heroic proportions had truth in it. Their biographers may have been able later to write accurately about their weaknesses and pettiness, but these have been transcended in death and the heroic portraits have become more true and real. In the spheres of spirit where ideals are true the souls of those still on earth and of those who have gone before can meet. Convincing experiences that this is so can develop out of mourning passed through and transcended. The inner loss becomes transformed into a gain. The experience of mourning can by its own nature pass through three stages. It begins with the descent into the darkness of grief. It goes on into the stage in which the lost one is found again in experiences of the soul. It grows into the third, in which the soul is uplifted to the heights of the spirit where the soul that has passed through death finds its true eternal being.

Losing someone older

It can be a great shock to know the loss of a father, mother, or older relative. It is the same if one loses one's grandparents or the teachers of one's first years at school. One has always known that they were older and would be liable to go first, but the experience of shock remains. These are people who have always been there since one could remember. They have given to life its stable structure. They have allowed one's self to be a little more care free, to be without the risk of having no-one to depend on. Even if in the meantime they have become old and confined, they have nevertheless always been there. Suddenly, or so it always seems, they are there no longer. They have escaped from their appointed places and will be emerging into new experiences and adventures. The burdens they carry have been dropped, to be picked up if they can by those who have depended on them. They were the older generation and now one is exposed to the experience of being without them and having to take their place.

Those who stand at a distance may take calmly the news that one of the old people has died. They may be able to see death as a release from pains and troubles and for the others a release from responsibility. But the experience is quite different for those who are near to them. Death may still have been a release. But those left behind who were close to them will be needing comfort and a period to absorb the experience of loss. An important piece of their life has died also. The memories of childhood take on a different character. A new relationship to the past evolves bit by bit, as it seems to withdraw further. The feeling about one's own personality undergoes a subtle change. Those who have been bereaved in this sense require consideration, part of which will consist in allowing them to dwell more than usual in the past, until the personality has re-formed. There again, if the experience is hurried over, the process of maturing, which is so much a part of it, will not take place. There is much need today for appreciating what it means to pass with patience through the experiences of life.

Losing the young

It is felt to be particularly grievous to lose someone who has not lived the full span of a lifetime. What of the years which he will not live through, the things he did not do, the words he will never say? What of the promise unfulfilled, the care given to his growing years, which seems to have come to nothing? Grief is made acute by disappointment. Why should such things happen? A story was once written about the mother of several children all but one of whom died before they grew up. She retired into the country and lived with her grief. After a long time she came to believe that she among all mothers, did not lose her children because she never experienced them growing up and leaving home. In one sense she had retreated into an unreal kind of consolation. In a higher sense it is true that those who die young take with them their promise, their enthusiasm, the forces they have not used. They had not had time to spoil themselves or their lives, to meet disappointment or to lapse from their first endeavour. If they did not live to mature, they also did not decline.

The young who die are bound to those who stay behind quite particularly through the sense of the future. They have taken with them so much unused will, so many undimmed ideas that they may be felt working from the future into the present. Those who are concerned to make a relationship to them which outlasts death, find it in the most real sense when they begin to undertake some enterprise that is not forced upon them but begins with an ideal. 'If I had not lost him I would never have done, said or thought what I am doing and saying now.' So the one speaks who has known the pain of loss of this kind. There is no growing apart as time goes on but a growing together, when the new relationship has developed in this way. The pain of loss cannot be ignored or passed over. It may last much longer than that brought by the death of someone old. But if the temptation is overcome to live with the young who have gone only in memories and regrets, if there is the courage to experience the future, the relationship can work powerfully into the doings of life. The one who has died in old age brings memories of the past but the one who has died young calls up the impulses for the future.

In a sense, to think of those who have died as they once were in the past can be misleading. Death tranforms. One grows nearer to the dead one by asking: what is he becoming now, how has he emerged into his new life? How shall we go on together? rather than how do we remember each other? Anyone who feels that such questions might bring a further sense of loss, can realise that the person he knew here, before he went ahead, was not the same through the years but was growing and developing. Do we not love each other, not for what we are but for what we are becoming? When someone dies he faces change of the highest kind and those who love him face it likewise, as they endeavour to make a continuing relationship to him.

Losing children

Are all children meant to grow up? Why do some children live for only a few years, some babies for a few days and some never breathe? How is the mother to be consoled for the lost baby and how are such questions to be faced at a time when abortion is so widely practised that the question arises: What about those who have thrown their babies away before they had a chance to live? In all these experiences when life ends as it begins there is the strongest kind of grief as such. The grown-ups encounter it as something that they must feel but which goes beyond their own feelings. They become aware of a grief coming from the strongest disappointment. The soul of the child is disappointed that the immense effort made to reach life in the body has come to nothing. Whether the grown-ups are prepared for it or not the force of the child's grief makes a strong impact upon themselves. There is something in their experience which no reasoning or good sense can change because they are feeling a force stronger than their own. They will not be left always mourning but they will have known something that they are very unlikely to forget. It is the magic of grief itself.

When the grief is included in the experiences of life it is less difficult to bear. When a child has died and the mother with the other children include him in their thoughts about the family, speak of him as one of themselves, the grief becomes less bitter. A sweetness enters the relationship of the members of the family to one another which the children who are growing up into a tough world cannot give. The family can seem to have a guardian angel who is always at hand. After the grief has worn itself out the sweetness can last long.

The disappointment of the soul whose body has been prevented from being born is liable to be of the bitterest. It casts a shadow of reproach over the grown-ups which, whether or not it is realised, causes a deep sense of wrong. There is a bitter harvest of confused feelings to be reaped at a time when the respect for human life on the one hand is flatly contradicted by so many, who on the other hand think of themselves as right minded people. Arguments may go to and fro, points of view clash but they do not touch the grief that pierces to the depths of the heart where the reality of experience is felt.

Bereavement is the experience of grief and those who wish to bring comfort cannot do so as onlookers but in the sharing of it. When grief is not avoided it lasts until it can be healed. Grief clears the mind and brings insight. But can it truly be said that it is valuable in itself? Everything depends upon how it is transformed. For it can be known by first hand experience that the forces of the spirit of Christ are at work in us when the touch of healing falls upon our grief.

7
Practical Problems
(as encountered today in Gt Britain)

Registration

When a death takes place, the next of kin or someone in a similar position, is responsible for going to the Registrar to register the death. A medical certificate made out by the doctor who attended the one who has died, either at home or in hospital, will have to be taken to the local Registry. It is usual when a cremation is required that the medical certificate carries two signatures.

After registering the death, the Registrar will provide a disposal certificate made out either for burial or cremation. This will be needed at once by the undertaker, who will not be able to arrange either a burial or a cremation without it. There is a further complication if the death is reported to the coroner, whose duty it is to hold an enquiry. This will always happen in case of accident, violence, industrial disease or any suspicious circumstances. It sometimes happens that the coroner is called in for reasons beyond those already mentioned, some of which may seem very strange to the relatives. But the coroner's office is a legal one, and his dictates have to be respected even if he orders investigations, including the post-mortem examination of the body. Those who dislike this kind of procedure on religious grounds will still find that they are dealing with the law of the land. If an inquest is ordered it is unavoidable. It is possible, though not usually necessary, for those involved to have a legal representative present at the inquest. Once the coroner has been called in, registration has to be delayed until his investigations are complete, which means the postponement of issue of the disposal certificate.

At the Registrar's office information will be given about the benefits available under the Social Services to those responsible for the funeral. A Death Grant can be claimed. A widow or widower can usually receive a pension for the first weeks until their future position is clarified. Forms will have to be filled in, but help will be available from the officials concerned.

The funeral

After the doctor and the Registrar have done their part, the arrangements for the funeral should be made with the undertaker. He will undertake most of the duties that follow, but he will require in advance the signature of the one who will be responsible for paying the bill. He will be prepared to answer all questions about probable cost and alternative choices. Cremation is at present usually cheaper than burial. In cities it is very difficult to ensure that a single grave will be provided and for how long. Most graves today have been used before in several layers. A crematorium does not always charge the same fee as any other one. At present a funeral cannot cost less than five hundred pounds, and often costs much more. It is better to discuss with the undertaker at once what services he has to offer and what they will cost.

The undertaker is able to perform many of the tasks connected with death. He will be able to arrange for the body to be laid out and to be removed to his own premises if this is desirable. He is usually able to provide a Chapel of Rest, where the body can be visited and flowers arranged. Although it is valuable to keep the body at home for the first three days, this is often impossible under modern conditions, especially when the death has taken place in hospital. The Chapel of Rest will be much more desirable than the hospital mortuary. The work of the undertaker is usually done today by people who show real consideration for the bereaved, and are willing to make arrangements which will make their situation easier. This may arise when it is necessary for the dead body to be identified or when the special procedures are involved which belong to deaths by accident, whether on land, at sea or in the air.

The undertaker will arrange all the details of the funeral and provide transport. He must of course know what the wishes are of those concerned. He should be instructed as to what ceremonies should be held at the crematorium or the graveside, by whom they should be carried out, and who is to be informed that he is required to hold the funeral service. He will then carry out the wishes which have been presented to him.

It is important that as soon as possible after the death the deceased's last will and testament should be found and read. It is always useful if the wishes of the deceased about the funeral are found recorded in his will. Those left behind can then feel satisfied that they are making decisions of which the decreased would approve. Where there is no will and no record of wishes, those concerned will be left to follow their own sense of right.

Bequeathing the body

It is open to everyone to bequeath his body for purposes of medical research. Such bequests are dealt with by the Inspector of Anatomy, 160 Great Portland Street, London W1N 5DT. Such bequests should be made in writing either in the will or in statements made to the executors. If such a bequest is accepted the medical school which uses the body will pay all funeral costs. The funeral will clearly take place much later, but bequeathing the body for medical research does not mean that a funeral is therefore excluded. Where the donor wishes to bequeath certain organs a special procedure is necessary. If these are kidneys or eyes for instance, they must be removed immediately after death. Such donors are required to carry a signed card with them so that their wishes can be known immediately.

It is of course a matter of principle which each one can only decide for himself whether to bequeath the body or not. To do so will certainly cause a certain disturbance to the soul, that has left the body, during the first days after death. Nevertheless, it is possible to feel that this would be part of a sacrifice worth while because it would contribute to the development of medical knowledge. On the other hand, there are those who will not agree that knowledge gained in this manner is really valuable.

Carrying out wishes

Making a will may seem a very tiresome job, but it will bring great benefit to those left behind. The help of the solicitor should be called upon, even though he must be paid a fee, to make sure that the declaration of wishes is valid. The will should include statements about all that is left, including details about valued personal possessions and good intentions towards friends as well as relatives. It is sometimes felt as hard to imagine, but in fact the one who dies will cease at death to have any control over what happens to his belongings or at his own funeral. But wishes stated in a will have legal force.

Among the variety of possible wishes is the matter of whether flowers are required at the funeral. They are sometimes considered to be a waste of money. In actual experience they add so much sweetness to what is often an occasion for grief, that a funeral without flowers can seem arid (the same goes for music). They confirm for those present the deep feeling that they meet in the soul of the deceased an experience of love and joy, quite different from the sad one of disposing of the outworn body. They are an outer expression of value to the heart, in spite of what it costs in money. There should be at every funeral conversation about the character and destiny of the one who has died. A funeral address can be made by a good speaker or by the minister holding the service. It is a valuable means of remembering the one who has left the body in his spiritual significance, so that the hearts of those present will be lifted up to the appreciation of his real spiritual value. At the end of this life and the beginning of the next the human soul is warmed and strengthened by genuine, right-minded appreciation. The soul will gain in confidence for the beginning of his new life beyond the Gate of Death.

Funerals and memorial services are important events. They are not just matters of outer observance. They are places of meeting between those left here on earth and the one who has gone ahead. The new relationship is being formed which will enrich the existence of both in the years to come. It is of the greatest importance to remember and consider those who have died, not ceasing to do so as the years pass. Whether or not remembering involves setting up tombstones, memorial plaques, or planting trees and bushes is a matter of choice. They are not of value in themselves, but are important to those who need a fixed point to which to attach their remembering. There are so many ways of remembering those who have died in so vital a way that they live on in the present and into the future as spiritual personalities to be included in the thoughts and feelings of those who are still in the body.

Afterthought

The human situation is changing because history is on the move. The question is: where is it going? Human nature is changing because man is a being in the process of development. A person can go back or forward but he cannot stand still. Mankind cannot stand still. Because there is a guardian of history, Chirst, who has taken this responsibility upon Himself, a way of progress opens ahead. But Christ is also the Guardian of freedom, and no one can go that way except out of his own will. The picture of that which is at the end of the road is the Holy City. It cannot be just found, it has to be built. This is the mystery of human life.